Thief

First published in 2007 by Cherrytree Books,
a division of the Evans Publishing Group
2A Portman Mansions
Chiltern St
London W1U 6NR

Design. D.R.ink

British Library Cataloguing in Publication Data
Amos, Janine
    Thief – (Good & Bad Series)
    I. Title II. Green, Gwen III. Series
    364.162

ISBN 1 84234 398 X
13 –digit ISBN (from 1 Jan 2007) 978 1 84234 398 2

Thief

By Janine Amos

Illustrated by Gwen Green

CHERRYTREE BOOKS

Ravi's story

The boys were sitting up against the park fence. Everyone was listening to Gareth. He was making a plan.

"We'll go to old Mr Baxter's shop," said Gareth. "We'll take sweets, crisps and comics. Some of those new felt pens, too."

They all watched Gareth as he stood up. He was a big boy with red hair. "We'll meet back here afterwards and share it out," he said. Then Gareth pointed straight at Ravi. "It's your turn today, Ravi."

"Oh, no," thought Ravi. He didn't want to take anything from Mr Baxter's shop. His heart started to beat very fast.

"I'll be look-out! Come on!" shouted Gareth. And the boys ran off. Slowly, Ravi followed them.

It was dark inside the shop. It smelt of chocolate and newspapers. Mr Baxter was behind the counter talking to a customer.

Ravi looked at the sweets. There were rows and rows of them. He swallowed hard. His throat was dry. Ravi heard Gareth coughing behind him. That was the signal to hurry up.

Ravi shot out his hand and grabbed at the sweets. He stuffed some into his jacket pocket. Ravi headed for the door. He was shaking. He didn't care about the crisps or the comics or the felt pens. He just wanted to get out of Mr Baxter's shop.

How is Ravi feeling

Ravi didn't go to the park to meet the others. He ran straight home. When he got there he was puffing. What if Mr Baxter were following him? Ravi felt awful.

Ravi's dad was in the kitchen. He was reading the newspaper. But he put it down when Ravi rushed in.

"Whatever's the matter with you?" asked Ravi's dad.

Ravi emptied his jacket pocket. He showed his dad the sweets he'd taken from Mr Baxter's shop. He lined the sweets up on the table.

"I wish I hadn't done it," said Ravi.

"And why did you?" asked his dad.

"Because the other boys do," said Ravi.

"That doesn't mean that you should!" said Ravi's dad. "You can think for yourself."

"I know," said Ravi.

How do you think Ravi feels now?

"When I was your age, I stole some apples," said Ravi's dad. "I took them from a farmer's tree – as a dare."

"What happened?" asked Ravi.

"My dad made me take them back and say I was sorry," smiled Ravi's dad. "He said it was part of growing up. Now you'll have to return those sweets to Mr Baxter."

"Oh, no!" said Ravi.

"I'll come with you," said Ravi's dad, getting his coat.

It took Ravi and his dad a long time to walk to the shop. Ravi didn't want to go. His legs were shaking. He held the sweets tightly in a paper bag.

Ravi's dad waited until the shop was empty. Then he spoke to Mr Baxter.

"My son has something to tell you," said Ravi's dad.

Mr Baxter was quiet while Ravi told him about the sweets. He frowned as he listened. He looked cross.

"I'm sorry," said Ravi.

What do you think Mr Baxter will say?

At last Mr Baxter spoke.

"Thank you for coming," he said. "I would have missed those sweets at the end of the week. That's when I do all my counting up. I would have known they'd been taken."

Ravi looked down.

"You won't do it again, will you?" asked Mr Baxter.

"Never!" said Ravi. And he meant it.

Feeling like Ravi

Stealing is about taking something away from someone else. Ravi didn't want to steal. He knew it was wrong. He did it to join in with the other boys. Have you ever felt like Ravi?

Carried away

Sometimes it's easy to get carried away by other people's ideas. They might try to make you think that stealing is fun or dare you to steal. They might call you names if you don't – or say that you can't be their friend.

Think for yourself

At times like this, it's important to remember that you have a mind of your own. It doesn't matter what others think. You must do what you know is right.

Think about it!

Read the stories in this book. Think about the people in the stories. You might have felt like them sometimes. You might have felt you wanted to steal – or someone may have tried to make you steal. Think what is the best thing to do if this happens to you.

Holly's story

"I won!" laughed Fay. Fay and her brother Simon raced to the armchair. Rusty the dog joined in, barking.

It was always noisy at Fay's house. Everyone always seemed to be laughing or talking at once. Even Fay's mum was noisy, with her big, loud voice.

Holly stood in the doorway and watched them. She always seemed to be at Fay's house these days. Holly's mum was in hospital. So Holly went to Fay's every day after school. She liked it there. But sometimes she felt a bit left out.

Holly wandered into the big front room. It was quiet in there. The sun was shining in through the window. And there was a bowl of flowers on the piano.

Holly closed the door softly behind her. This was Fay's mum's special place. There were brightly coloured rugs on the floor. And under the window was Fay's mum's collection of dolls. They came from all around the world.

Holly went to stand in front of them. There was one doll that Holly liked more than all the others. It was the smallest one of all. It had a white lace dress with tiny gold buttons.

Holly could hear Fay giggling in the next room. Just then, Holly wanted the doll very much. She slowly picked it up. Holly took out a tissue and carefully wrapped up the little doll. Then she slipped it into her pocket.

"Holly! Tea's ready!" called Fay's mum. Holly ran through to the kitchen. She could feel the doll in her pocket. It bumped against her as she moved.

Holly was quiet all through tea. Simon told a silly story. But he couldn't make her laugh.

Fay's mum was worried. "Are you feeling ill, Holly?" she asked.

Holly shook her head. She wasn't ill – but she wasn't very happy, either.

What's the matter with Holly?

How do you think she feels?

After tea, Holly helped to clear the table. She stood up to pass her plate, and out fell the doll, in front of everyone. Simon and Fay stopped laughing. They stared at the doll and they stared at Holly. Holly went bright red.

Quickly, Fay's mum picked up the doll. "Let's go into the front room, Holly," she said. "Let's have a chat."

What do you think will happen

Holly followed Fay's mum into the front room. Fay's mum closed the door behind them.

"You took my doll without asking," said Fay's mum.

Holly looked down at her toes. "I'm sorry," she said. But her voice wasn't working very well. Holly thought that she might cry.

"That's stealing, Holly," said Fay's mum. "Why did you do it?"

"I don't know," said Holly, truthfully.

Fay's mum put her arms round Holly and gave her a big hug.

"I wish my mum was home," said Holly quietly. "I wish she wasn't in hospital."

"I know," said Fay's mum. "But things will get better soon. You'll see."

Fay's mum held out the little doll. "Now, you can borrow any of my dolls — but you must ask first. OK?"

"OK," said Holly.

"And I'm always here if you want a chat," said Fay's mum. "Talking always helps."

Is Fay's mum right?

Feeling like Holly

Have you ever felt like Holly? Have you ever wanted to steal from someone you know well? Holly couldn't say why she took the doll. Sometimes it's hard for people to know exactly why they do things.

Talking helps

Sometimes people steal because they are worried about something. Perhaps they feel lonely or upset. If you're worried, like Holly, try talking about it. Talk to an adult you trust.

Tim's story

Tim was in the kitchen reading his comic. He could hear his mum talking on the phone.

"And it's my birthday on Saturday," Tim's mum was saying. Tim started to listen.

"No, I'm not doing anything," his mum went on. "I'll have a quiet night in, as usual."

Tim's mum laughed. But it wasn't a proper laugh. She didn't sound happy. Tim looked across at his mum. He wondered how old she was. She had lines on her face and she looked tired.

"She needs cheering up," thought Tim. "I'll make her birthday special. I'll get her a really great present."

After school the next day, Tim went shopping.

"I'll buy Mum's birthday card first," he thought.

There were lots of cards in the shop. And it took Tim ages to choose. At last he found one. There was no price on the card. But when Tim took it to the till he had a shock. It was very expensive. Slowly, Tim handed over the money. It was almost all he had.

Tim walked on through the big shop, looking for a present. He saw some boxes of chocolates. But he couldn't afford them.

Next, Tim went to the perfume counter. His mum loved perfume! Tim looked at the rows of coloured bottles. He bent to sniff one.

"Don't touch!" said the assistant, crossly.

Tim moved off. Perfume was expensive, anyway.

What would you do if you were Tim?

It was getting late. Tim started to worry.

"I'll never find anything here," he thought. "Everything costs too much."

Just then, Tim saw some scarves. They were hanging up right in front of him. He looked around – no one was watching. Quickly, Tim pulled down a bright, blue scarf. He pushed it deep into his pocket.

When Tim got home, he went straight to his room. He found some old wrapping paper and wrapped up the scarf. The parcel wasn't very neat. Tim's hands were shaking too much. He felt a bit sick. Tim hid the parcel under his bed. He tried not to think about it. He tried to forget what he'd done.

How do you think Tim is feeling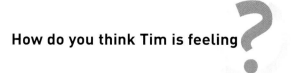

Tim woke early next morning. His mum was still in bed.

"Happy birthday!" shouted Tim, running into her room.

Tim's mum read the card first. Then she opened the parcel. She took out the long, blue scarf.

"It's lovely!" said Tim's mum, stroking it with one finger. Tim grinned.

Then Tim's mum put the scarf down on the bed.

"This is real silk," she said. "Where did you get the money?"

Tim didn't know what to say.

"Oh, Tim," said his mum, "please don't tell me it's stolen!"

Tim didn't answer.

Tim's mum went very quiet. Tim knew she was crying. He felt his own eyes fill up with tears.

Then Tim's mum put her arm round him.

"Promise me you won't ever do this again," she said.

Tim nodded.

"Things don't make me happy," said Tim's mum. "I'd much rather you made me a cup of coffee as a present – or did me a painting."

After a while, Tim stood up.

"Where are you going?" asked his mum.

"To put the coffee on," said Tim, quietly.

What will Tim's mum do with the scarf?

Feeling like Tim

Have you ever felt like Tim? Have you ever wanted something that you couldn't afford? It's sometimes hard to accept that you can't have something you badly want. It's sometimes easy to think that a big shop wouldn't miss it. But stealing is wrong, even from big shops.

Counting the cost

Tim was only trying to make his mum happy. Instead, he made her cry. She didn't want him to be a thief. And she didn't want a present that cost a lot of money. Just because something costs a lot, it doesn't mean someone will like it more.

Yours to give

A present has to be yours to give. The scarf didn't belong to Tim. It wasn't his to give. But there are plenty of other things Tim could have given his mum. He could have done a painting. He could have made her breakfast. He could have done the washing up.

Thinking about stealing

Ravi, Holly and Tim each took something that didn't belong to them. And they each learnt something about stealing. Think about the stories in this book. What are the things that you've learnt?

If you are feeling frightened or unhappy, don't keep it to yourself. Talk to an adult you can trust, like a parent or a teacher. If you feel really alone, you could telephone or write to one of these offices. Remember, there is always someone who can help.

Childline
Freephone 0800 1111
Address: Freepost 1111, London N1 0BR

Childline for children in care
Freephone 0800 884444 (6 - 10pm)
www.childline.org.uk

NSPCC Child Protection Line
Freephone 0808 8005000
www.nspcc.org.uk

The Samaritans
08457 909090
www.samaritans.org.uk